Funeral Service For Jesus

A Service For Good Friday

Roy Caudill

CSS Publishing Company, Inc., Lima, Ohio

Copyright © 1997 by
CSS Publishing Company, Inc.
Lima, Ohio

ISBN 0-7880-1137-5   PRINTED IN U.S.A.

Each year Christian churches seek to portray in some way the story of the death and resurrection of Jesus. This Good Friday presentation offers a creative approach, bringing new power to the observance of a timeless, historic event.

Roy Braxton Caudill is currently pastor of the United Church of Canistota, South Dakota, an ecumenical parish of United Methodists and Presbyterians. After serving in the United States Air Force in aircraft maintenance for 20 years, he entered seminary and earned the Master of Divinity degree from North American Baptist Seminary, Sioux Falls, South Dakota. He and his wife Lazann are the parents of two daughters.

*To the glory
of God*

Introduction

This service places the death of Jesus in a contemporary scene. This is accomplished by conducting a funeral service for Jesus following the format for a contemporary funeral service in a local church. A casket should be placed at the front of the church. It should be closed and locked so no one can open it. A local funeral home will probably provide the casket free of charge. Near the casket on an easel should be a picture of Jesus. The service should be held at approximately 3:00 p.m. on Good Friday. If your church has a tradition of serving a lunch or other refreshments following a funeral service, then provide for that and a time of fellowship following the service.

A few days before the service have a notice printed in the local paper. Memorial folders should also be printed for those attending the service. Your funeral director may provide them free of charge. Samples of the newspaper announcement and memorial folder are provided.

Remember, the goal is to duplicate, as nearly as possible, the traditions of your church when a death occurs.

Note: The Good Friday worship service reflects that Jesus has died. Resurrection has not yet occurred. All scriptures and songs must apply Old Testament images, other than the gospel which describes Jesus' death.

Order Of Service

Good Friday

Prelude

Greetings/Words Of Grace

*Gospel Lesson   Luke 23:44-56

*Hymn   "Abide With Me"

Opening Prayer

Scripture   Psalm 22; Genesis 22:1-8

Special Music *(Choir)*   "God Provides The Lamb"[1]

Message   "Will God Provide A Lamb?"

Special Music *(Choir)*   "Behold Calvary's Lamb"[2]

Commendation

Lord God, he is gone. He loved us. We loved him, but you took
him away. Why have you forsaken us? God of heaven, hear these
words from our shattered and trembling hearts. You are always
God. You give and you take away. You gave Jesus to us; now you
have reclaimed him. Where we doubt, give us light; strengthen us
in our weakness; show mercy where we have sinned; where we
sorrow, give us your peace. We give Jesus back to you. Raise him
up if it would be within your will. Love him and love us. Help us to
love you in spite of this, and because of this. Give us the ability to
trust and to continue to serve you in this world as we wait to enter
your joy in the world to come. Amen.

Announcement
(The following announcement should be made if the Sunrise Service, He Is Not Here, *will be used.)*
Due to the lateness of the hour, and the fact that the Sabbath is almost upon us, the committal service will be delayed until Sunday morning. Join us here *(state the location)* at *(time)*.

*Closing Hymn   "O Love That Will Not Let Me Go"

*Benediction
May God bless you and keep you
May God's face shine upon you
      and be gracious to you.
May God look upon you with kindness
      and give you peace. Amen.

*Postlude

*Please stand if able

———————

1. Source: *Alone On The Altar: Calvary's Lamb.* Created by Randy Vader and Jay Rouse, Praise Gathering Music, 1995.
   Note: If no choir is available, have the congregation sing "Were You There?".
   Sing all verses except the last.

2. Source: *Alone On The Altar*, Praise Gathering Music, 1995.
   Note: If no choir is available, have the congregation sing "Beneath The Cross of Jesus" or another appropriate hymn.

Sermon

Thirty-three years go by so fast. Why, it seems as if it were only yesterday that wise men were bringing and angels were singing, as we welcomed the child Jesus into the world. Thirty years later, the child became a man. For three years we walked with him. It was so exciting watching him calm storms, heal the sick, raise the dead, and usher in a kingdom built on faith in him. But these last forty days have shaken us. Lent came and

> *When Lent comes,*
> * you have to put away the tinsel;*
> *you have to take down your Christmas tree,*
> * and stand out in the open ... vulnerable.*
> *You either are or you aren't.*
> *You either believe or you don't.*
> *You either will or you won't.*
> *And, O Lord, how we love the stables and the star!*
> *When Lent comes the angels' voices*
> * begin their lamenting,*
> *and we find ourselves in a courtyard*
> * where we must answer*
> *whether we know him or not.*
> — From "Kneeling in Jerusalem," by Ann Weems,
> Westminster/John Knox, 1992

Now it is Friday. The forty days have ended. It is dark, for the light that was in the world, and in our lives, has been snuffed. Jesus of Nazareth has died. Were we mistaken about him? Was our faith in vain? We so wanted to believe that he really was the Messiah.

I'll never forget when the South Dakota Annual Conference was being held in Rapid City many years ago. All the churches from Sioux Falls to Mitchell decided to caravan to the conference. Six vans full of clergy, laity, and their families traveled together to the Black Hills. It was a special time. For five days we worshiped, conducted church business, and played together. We were on our way home when we stopped at "Al's Oasis" on the beautiful

9

Missouri River at Chamberlain, South Dakota. There we planned to refuel the vehicles and nourish ourselves. After we stepped out of the vans, Mary and Joseph asked together, "Where's Jesus?" They thought he was in one of the other vans. Others thought that Mary and Joseph should have kept a better watch over their child. After a quick investigation it was decided that Jesus had been left behind in Rapid City. So, we até hurriedly, and rearranged rides so that some of us would return to Rapid City with Mary and Joseph. We were worried. We couldn't get there fast enough. Upon entering the city, we went straight to Howard Johnson's, the site of the conference. Jesus wasn't there. We knew that the cabinet was meeting at the First United Methodist Church. Maybe they had seen him, or at least could help us locate him.

Imagine our surprise when the church secretary directed us to a meeting room where we found the boy Jesus sitting there with the bishop and five district superintendents. Jesus listened intently as the cabinet responded to his inquiries. The cabinet was amazed at Jesus' response to their comments, at his understanding of theological and practical matters of life and faith. So were we.

As a man, Jesus met and ministered to many people. Remember the time he was walking through the city park and a man named Zach wanted to see him? Being small in stature, Zach ran ahead of Jesus and climbed up into a tree. Maybe it was the leaf falling, a rustling in the branches, or a shadow on the ground that caught his attention. Maybe it was his wonderful awareness of everything that went on around him. Whatever it was, it caught his attention. He stopped, looked up, and said, "Zacchaeus!" Notice that Jesus always addressed people properly. He didn't cut them or their name short. He made them feel tall. "Zacchaeus, you come down, for I am going to your house today."

Zach couldn't believe it. Neither could we. Jesus pursuing the IRS man! That's the last person we would want to visit. See him and you receive no refund. In fact, you would pay more taxes. It was rumored that he even skimmed money off the top to line his own pocket. Yet Jesus gave him more than he deserved. "I'm going to your house today," Jesus said. It made us think, and it made the tax man think, too.

Not only did we think, we began to
he said, "The Father and I are one." "J
raise it up in three days." He wanted
illustrated it for us.

The widow of Nain's son ha
held at the church. The pastor '
lowed by six pallbearers carrying
was the grief-stricken mother. A large c.
her, helping her to bear this burden. At that m.
along with some of his followers. When he saw the
woman, he said, "Don't cry." Then he went up and touc..
coffin. Everyone stood still. Jesus said, "Young man, I say to you,
get up."

No one moved except the widow's son. He sat up and began to
speak. Jesus gave him back to his mother.

If that wasn't enough to fill us with hope, Lazarus certainly did
the trick, until ... until Jesus was arrested. We watched as he was
taken to Annas and Caiaphas, then to Pilate, to Herod, and back to
Pilate. It was a mockery. He was stripped and scourged with a whip
of leather straps that had metal and bone at the ends. The bone tore
at his flesh; the metal bruised deeply, as he was struck on the back,
buttocks, and legs. Nine straps, 39 lashes, for a total of 351 times
that his body was torn and bruised. And then, to add insult to in-
jury, he was struck in the face, spit upon, and finally crowned with
a crown of thorns which was forced down upon his head, before he
was led away to be nailed to a cross, where he died in agony.

There is nothing pretty or inviting about him now. That is why
the coffin is closed. We couldn't look at him then; we can't look at
him now. He is gone, and gone with him is our hope. He could not,
or would not, save himself. Now, we are left alone. What are we to
do? If he, who was life, could not live, how can we? It seems we
have two choices.

In the night
  when our world dissolves in tears
we feel
          abandoned.

knows
nobody understands
and nobody feels
our pain.
Even the ones who care
don't care
the way
we do.

In that moment
when there is no sound
and there is no sight,
nothing but the silent unrelenting night ...
in that moment
comes the choice
of Death or Life:
We can look down into our own Self
or we can look up to God,
the only star in our unlit skies.
— From "Searching For Shalom," by Ann Weems,
Westminster/John Knox Press, 1991

There it is. We can look down at this death before us, or, like Abraham, we can look to God. He who had been promised descendants as numerous as the stars in the sky willingly placed his only son on a sacrificial altar, trusting God to fulfill a promise even in the face of death. Abraham raised his hand, knife waiting to plunge into human flesh, but a rustle in the bushes stilled the moment. God provided a sacrifice, a ram was offered, and a son was returned from death.

But Jesus, Jesus has really died. He committed his life into the hands of his Father. We must do the same as we give him up to God. Our only question: Will God give him back? Will God provide a Lamb?

Funeral Services To Be Held For Jesus

Jesus, son of Mary, and Joseph (so people thought), was born in Bethlehem of Judea. At about the age of two he moved with his family to Egypt. At the age of four, he moved to the town of Nazareth in Galilee. Thus he was known the rest of his life as a Nazarene. He grew in wisdom and stature, and in favor with God and men. His young adult years were spent applying himself in the carpenter's trade. At age thirty he was baptized in the Jordan River and began a public ministry which progressed from Galilee into all of Judea. His ministry attracted large crowds who came to hear him preach, and to be healed. The people who gathered were witnesses to many miracles. After three years his ministry came to an abrupt end when he was accused of crimes against the state, claiming to be something that others said he was not. Jesus loved God and us. On a Friday afternoon he humbled himself and became obedient, even to death, death upon a cross. He had attained the age of 33 years.

Jesus is survived by his mother Mary; brothers James, Joseph, Simon, and Judas; and a number of sisters. He was preceded in death by his earthly father Joseph.

Funeral services will be held at the United Church of Canistota on Friday, April 10th, at 3:00 p.m.

Jesus, son of Mary, and Joseph (so people thought), was born in Bethlehem of Judea. At about the age of two he moved with his family to Egypt. At the age of four, he moved to the town of Nazareth in Galilee. Thus he was known the rest of his life as a Nazarene. He grew in wisdom and stature, and in favor with God and men. His young adult years were spent applying himself in the carpenter's trade. At age thirty he was baptized in the Jordan River and began a public ministry which progressed from Galilee into all of Judea. His ministry attracted large crowds who came to hear him preach, and to be healed. The people who gathered were witnesses to many miracles. After three years his ministry came to an abrupt end when he was accused of crimes against the state, claiming to be something that others said he was not. Jesus loved God and us. On a Friday afternoon he humbled himself and became obedient, even to death, death upon a cross. He had attained the age of 33 years.

Jesus is survived by his mother Mary; brothers James, Joseph, Simon, and Judas; and a number of sisters. He was preceded in death by his earthly father Joseph.

In Memory Of
Jesus

Date of birth
6 B.C.

Date of Death
27 A.D.

Funeral Service
Friday, April 10, 1998
3:00 p.m.
United Church of Canistota
Canistota, SD

Clergy
Rev. Roy Caudill

Organist
Starlyn Church

**Special Music by the
United Church Choir**
God Provides The Lamb
Behold Calvary's Lamb

Congregational Hymns
Abide With Me
O Love That Will Not Let Me Go

Peter: *(Walking up to the group)* Hey! What's going on?

First Reader: We want to prepare Jesus' body for burial. The pastor unlocked the coffin, but nobody wants to open it.

Peter: Is that all? I'll do it. *(Slowly opens coffin)*

Third Reader: *(Astonished)* He's gone!

Fifth Reader: How can that be? The pastor had the only key.

Pastor: I never opened it. I was observing the Sabbath like the rest of you. I swear on the Holy Scriptures that I did not touch it. Besides, we had guards posted all weekend, and the church was locked.

Peter: Look at this! The burial cloth. It's folded so neatly. And the head linens, the same way.

Sixth Reader
(Female): *(Running up to the group)* I was out there in the garden. *(Points toward the trees east of the church)* I saw a man. I thought it was the gardener. But when he spoke to me I realized it was our Lord! *(Loudly with excitement)* HE'S ALIVE!

(All fall to their knees in praise and worship.)

Closing Prayer or
Solo   "Because He Lives I Can Face Tomorrow"

The End

Fifth Reader

(Female): The pastor said there would be a committal service later this morning. The first thing we need to do is prepare the body for burial, then we'll decide what to do with the rest of our lives. I brought some spices and new linens.

Second Reader: Martha, you are the most organized person I have ever known.

Third Reader: Do you realize it's been three days since he died? And besides, the coffin has been closed and sealed. The pastor has the only key.

First Reader: I'll go get him. Maybe he'll open it for us. *(Brings the pastor forward)*

Pastor: I understand that you want to prepare the body for this morning's burial?

Fifth Reader: Yes. Would you unlock the coffin for us?

Pastor: Well, I guess that would be all right. We do have time before the service. *(The pastor unlocks the coffin.)* There you are. Go ahead and open it.

First Reader: *(Stepping back)* Not me. *(To the second reader)* You do it.

Second Reader: Not me. *(To the third reader)* You do it.

Third Reader: Don't look at me. *(To fourth reader)* You do it.

Fourth Reader: Ohhhh no you don't. *(To fifth reader)* You do it.

Fifth Reader: No way! Look! Here comes Peter. Maybe he will open it.

He Is Not Here
(Skit)

First Reader
(Male): I still can't believe he's gone.

Second Reader
(Male): I know what you mean. Who would have ever thought that death would stop him?

Third Reader
(Female): I remember how he spoke to me at the well. He promised me living water. He said he was the Messiah. More than anything in the world I wanted it to be true. *(Sadly)* But now he's gone.

Fourth Reader
(Female): I know what you mean. I was the one that others caught in the act of adultery. They were about to hurl stones at me. It meant certain death. But Jesus, *(pause)* he said: "You who are without sin cast the first stone." Then he looked at the ground and began to write in the dirt. I couldn't believe what happened next. The men slowly put down their stones and walked away. When Jesus looked up, I was the only one left. I thought, "He's going to let me have it now." But instead, he looked at me and said, "Go and sin no more." I have never known such love. Ever since, my life has been so different. I wish I could have thanked him, but now he's gone.

First Reader: Yes, he's gone. I couldn't believe he allowed himself to die that way. He never did a thing to save himself. Even told Peter to put down his sword. No violence allowed except that done to him. He gave in to it all.

Second Reader: That's all true, but it's behind us now. The question is: Where do we go from here?

Sunrise Service

Prelude

Praise Singing
(Youth singing alone or have congregation join in)

Opening Hymn   "Morning Has Broken"

Opening Prayer
(Congregation in unison or prayed by youth)

Scripture   John 20:1-18

Hymn   "In The Garden"

Message   "He Is Not Here"
(Youth Skit)

Closing Hymn   "Alleluia"

(During the singing of the last hymn, Jesus appears in the distance. He stands there, with arms outstretched, blessing the people. He is gone by the time the singing ends.)

6

Introduction

This service is set in a contemporary format. It works well to allow the youth of the church to lead the service and play the parts. However, others can perform the parts just as well.

All participants should dress in contemporary clothing, what one wears on a regular basis. You will need a locked coffin at the front of the church. A local funeral home will probably provide one free of charge. The pastor should have the key to the coffin. You will need two male readers, four female readers, and one person to play the part of Peter, in addition to the pastor.

The service will take 30 to 45 minutes. Scripts and order of service are provided.

This Easter Sunrise Service is intended to be used as a follow-up to the Good Friday presentation, *A Funeral Service For Jesus.* The service is set in a contemporary format. The coffin that was placed in the front of the church on Good Friday remains at the front of the church. The pastor holds the key.

Seven participants are required to conduct this 30- to 45-minute service.

Church members, young and old, have found these two services to be the most gripping and meaningful Holy Week commemorations they have ever experienced.

Roy Braxton Caudill is currently pastor of the United Church of Canistota, South Dakota, an ecumenical parish of United Methodists and Presbyterians. After serving in the United States Air Force in aircraft maintenance for 20 years, he entered seminary and earned the Master of Divinity degree from North American Baptist Seminary, Sioux Falls, South Dakota. He and his wife Lazann are the parents of two daughters.

HE IS NOT HERE

ISBN 0-7880-1137-5

PRINTED IN U.S.A.

He Is
Not Here

An Easter Sunrise Service

Roy Caudill

CSS Publishing Company, Inc., Lima, Ohio